Clawed Monet's

Book

of

Famous Cats

**HOWELL
BOOK
HOUSE**

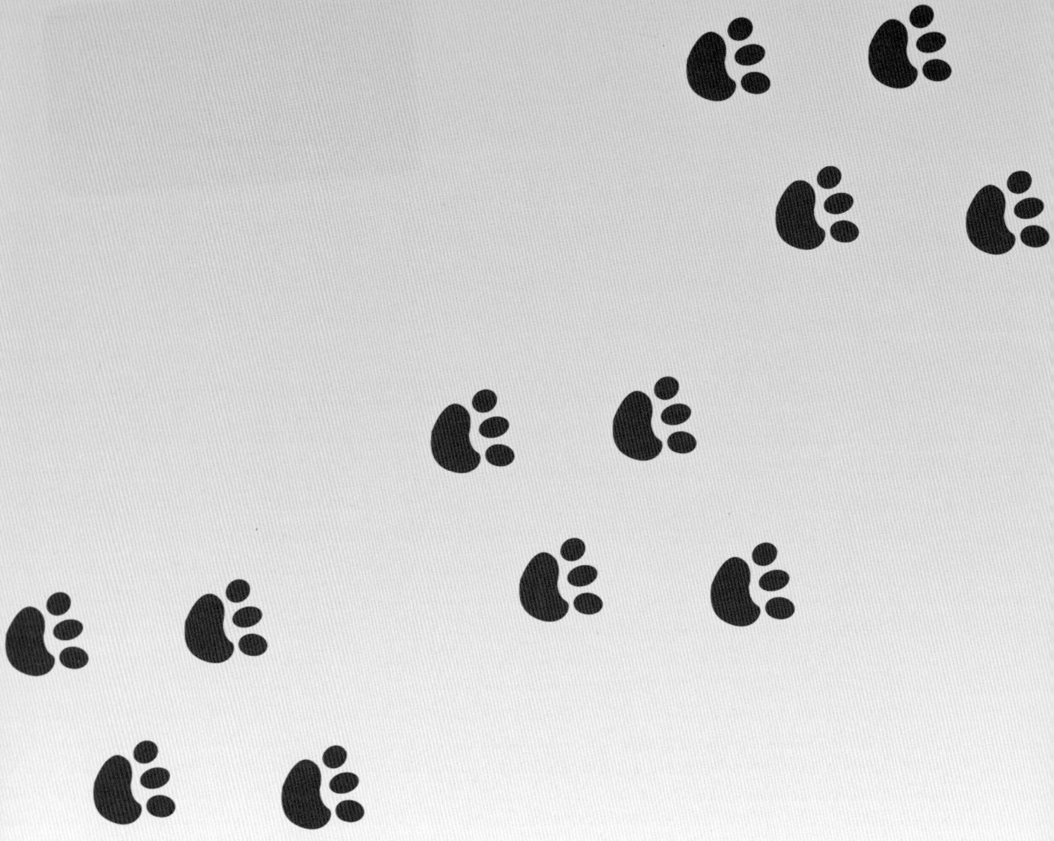

Clawed Monet's Book of Famous Cats
PEARL LAU

Howell Book House
Copyright © 1996 by Pearl Lau.

Howell Book House
A Simon & Schuster Macmillan Company
1633 Broadway
New York, NY 10019

MACMILLAN is a registered trademark of Macmillan, Inc.
Library of Congress Cataloging-in-Publication Data

Lau, Pearl.
Clawed Monet's book of famous cats / Pearl Lau with Clawed Monet.
p.   cm.
ISBN 0-87605-087-9
1. Cats—Literary collections. 2. Cats—Humor.
I. Title.
PN6071/C3L38 1996
818'.5407—dc20

Manufactured in the United States of America
10 9 8 7 6 5 4 3 2 1

Dedication

Thanks to Marcy Zingler, my editor, who listened to stories of my big cat Clawed, and pushed me along.

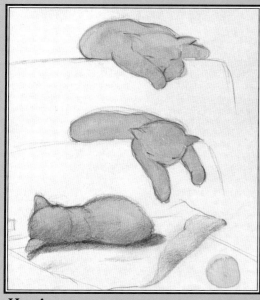

Here's sketches of me (Clawed) as a baby. Cute, Huh?

Thanks to Sean Frawley, publisher of Howell Book House who trusted all of us to finish the project. Thanks to Alan Oakes, former president of Macmillan, who signed off on the project (but had to tease me *a lot* before he did). Thanks to Richard Fox, who helped find terrific cat objets. Thanks to my mom who paid for my art lessons as a kid and always bought me new markers. Thanks to my husband Richard Comerford who kept the computer going. Thanks to my daughter Lily for just being. And thanks to my big cat Clawed, who if he was a person, would be out partying right now.

Cat Contents

Introduction

CATS
NEED
NO
INTRODUCTION. The first feral cat walked inside a cave and – duh – found it warmer and drier. People will tell you they let us stay with them and will recount stories of our being good mousers (true), eating rats from medieval tables (true), and helping the Japanese protect stored grain (true).

But just remember, we moved indoors because it's easier.

People don't win today in the brain department, but back in B.C., oh boy, was life rich! In Egypt, they thought gods manifested themselves in feline form. They even thought we were under the protective influence of the sun and the moon. When the Egyptians rubbed their hands on us and got sparks, they thought we were responsible for fire, and that we were giving off solar expressions. When our eyes changed and glowed, they thought it was due to the phases of the moon, and we could bestow power to those who worshiped us.

Would *you* have dissuaded them?

There are paintings and carvings of us from Cyprus, Crete, India, China, and the pre-Colombian types of the New World. Cats are travelers; the saying goes, we're "always on the wrong side of the door." We like to move! The world is big! So, we traveled and got ourselves worshiped in the weirdest places. In Mexico, the Mayans and the Aztecs mounted our faces on temples, warriors' breastplates, and household items similar to those cute little spoon rests in your kitchy-kitchen.

Can you say "Tepeyollotli"? That's an Aztec cat carved into Aztec calendars.

"Why do we have nine lives?" you may ask. Early worshippers thought of three as the mystic holy number, the trinity, the sacred symbol for mother, father, child. The figure three also represented the moon passing around the earth, as shown in hieroglyphics. Eventually they got around to three times three, or the Trinity of Trinities, and that equaled nine. In addition, when curled up, we cats create a circle (there's that sun and moon thing again), which has a mathematical formula of 360 degrees, or $3 + 6 + 0 = 9$. They really loved nine, they really loved cats, so they gave us the highest honor: nine lives.

Or so the legend goes.

Cats make exquisite photographs…they don't keep bouncing at you to be kissed just as you get the lens adjusted.

—Gladys Tabor

Cats as Marketing Tools

An advertising card from 1839 England promises many delights. Among them are cats who strike upon an anvil, ring bells, grind knives, roast coffee, beat a drum, turn a spit, play music, and grind rice in the Italian manner. It goes on to say, "the cleverest cat draws water from a well."

The dog can only play dominoes.

Bartholomew Fair.

THE Greatest Wonder in England IS

THE LEARNED

CATS!

SIGNOR CAPPELLI

(Previous to his leaving London) begs leave most respectfully to inform the Visitors and Inhabitants of the Metropolis, that having met the most flattering encouragement while in Regent-street, London, Brighton, Bath, Cheltenham, Manchester, Liverpool, Dublin, Edinburgh, &c. &c. where he has been patronised by the Nobility and Gentry, will now exhibit his WONDERFUL AMUSEMENTS,

Performed by Cats,

At 19, GILTSPUR STREET,

EVERY DAY

DURING THE FAIR.

We can sell anything. Soap is obvious; we are fastidiously clean. Nineteenth century merchants used little colorful cards as a reminder of their products. But a fish-wielding monkey teasing a cat to demonstrate the strength of thread is a stretch.

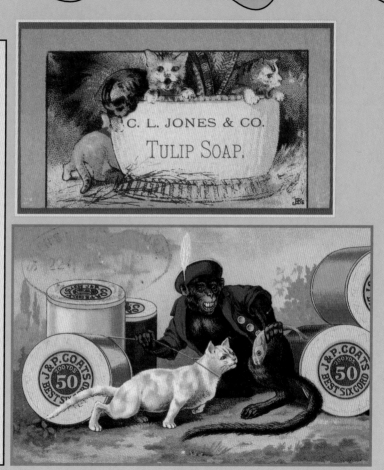

Sure, sure, it's the "ol black cat made me buy it" line. This black cat symbol is on everything from tobacco to shoe heels to German wine. True, we're influential, true, we're great–and handsome beyond imagination! In England (where the sun never sets on the empire) it's bad luck if a cat crosses your path. In Japan (land of the rising sun) it's good luck to have a black cat. Maybe it's all in the timing. It's good luck when you own one of us, but bad luck if we walk in front of someone, namely a quarrelsome neighbor.

14

Edward Penfield drew countless posters of us cats between the late 1800s and 1925, when he died. This May 1896 cover for *Harper's* shows two very smiley felines. Personally, I hate to be held that way—it makes my stomach stick out.

In the 11th century, St. Ives was the patron saint of lawyers (they need a patron saint?). He was always depicted with a cat, the symbol of justice. Here, La Liberté, stands in 1804. She's chained, but "freedom" is represented by, who else? This French Revolutionary engraving is of the Emblem after Prudhon, from Les Chats by Champfleury. The French really know how to treat us cats; we're even allowed in Paris restaurants. Oui, Oui!

Morris made ginger cats famous! People fell for the finicky cat thing. Bragging about your cat's habits is like saying you have the best doctor. "I got the worst doctor, and my cat'll eat anything." (Who would say *that*?) This famous 14-pound tabby came from a shelter in Chicago and was discovered by his owner/trainer. Morris was an award-winning spokescat from 1968 until 1978, when the first Morris passed away. A brand-new Morris has currently convinced advertisers to generate an entire new campaign around his impressive likeness.

There may be more to life than eating and sleeping, but I hope not.

I'd like mornings better if they started later.

Ah, Garfield, my Garfield—best-selling author and marketing genius. Mugs, posters, telephones, towels—you name it, his moniker is plastered on it. Everyone who wants to sleep, eat lasagna, or can't be bothered with much else, identifies with Garfield. As my mentor, he has the most widely syndicated strip since 1978. He also has over 33 books, with 11 of them hitting the number one spot on the *New York Times* best-seller list. Not bad for a lazy cat and his drawing person, Jim Davis, the brilliant creator of a character who people can relate to in 26 languages.

Dogs are nature's way of telling us we could be worse off.

Diet is "Die" with a "T".

19

I and Pangur Ban my cat,
'Tis a like task we are at:
Hunting mice is his delight,
Hunting words I sit all night.

Better than praise of men
'Tis to sit with book and pen;
Pangur bears me no ill will,
He too plies his simple skill.

'Tis a merry thing to see
At our tasks how glad are we,
When at home we sit and find
Entertainment to our mind.

Oftentimes a mouse will stray
In the hero Pangur's way;
Oftentimes my keen thought set
Takes a meaning in its net.

Translated by
Robin Flower

'Gainst the wall he sets his eye
Full and fierce and sharp and sly;
'Gainst the wall of knowledge I
All my little wisdom try.

When a mouse darts from its den
O how glad is Pangur then!
O what gladness do I prove
When I solve the doubts I love!

So in peace our tasks we ply,
Pangur Ban, my cat and I;
In our arts we find our bliss,
I have mine and he has his.

Practice every day has made
Pangur perfect in his trade;
I get wisdom day and night
Turning darkness into light.

This 9th Century poem and 16th century German Crest come from the same mind. In other words, we cats like to EAT.

Cats are intended to teach us that not everything in nature has a function •

Garrison Keillor

–American author and humorist, 1948–

Though such things may appear to carry a bit of fiction with them, it may be depended on that the pupils of her eyes seem to fill up and grow large with the full moon and to decrease and diminish again in brightness on its waning.

–Plutarch– 46?-120? A.D., Greek biographer and historian

The Egyptians believed that cats waxed and waned also.
One of the earliest likenesses of a cat appears in a cave in Dordogne, France. (There's those ailurophiles [cat lovers] again.) This Egyptian depiction dates from 1,500 B.C. Note: B.C. does NOT mean *before cats*.

Oh those Egyptians! Believing in the afterlife supported a whole embalming industry. There was probably a union, and they were hardly planning on letting everyone know there might not be an after-life.

The cat goddess Bast (or Ubastet, or Bubastis, or Pasht, as she was called) was considered the daughter of Isis, and loved by Ra, that cool sun god.

Having an old-age cat in the house meant good luck. This certainly was good luck for cats.

In 1890, three hundred thousand cat mummies were found by archeologists in Ben Hasser. The site was a former temple dedicated to Bastet. The cats had mummified mice buried with them! When Egyptian families had ill children, the parents would shave their own heads and sell the hair for gold and silver. The money would be given as an offering to sacred cats. The family would stay at the temple and study the cat, hoping they would receive a sign of their child's recovery.

What could they have used this for in the olden' days? Cat decoy by the mouse hole? Then jump on the unsuspecting mouse when he tries to sneak out of another hole? You can find this decoy and the salt-glaze cats in Colonial Williamsburg. Perhaps a founding father owned them?

If a cat spoke, it would say things like, "Hey I don't see the problem here."

—Roy Blount, Jr., American author

Even with a mouse on his face? This early American salt-glaze pair was someone's idea of a joke... I guess.

27

SHE: The cat has eaten our pet bird;
HE: Then the wicked beast shall die.
Then he resumed his quail on toast.
And she ate pigeon pie.

–Unknown

A Roman tabby mosaic from Pompeii, circa A.D. 87.
When in or near Rome, do as Roman kitties do.

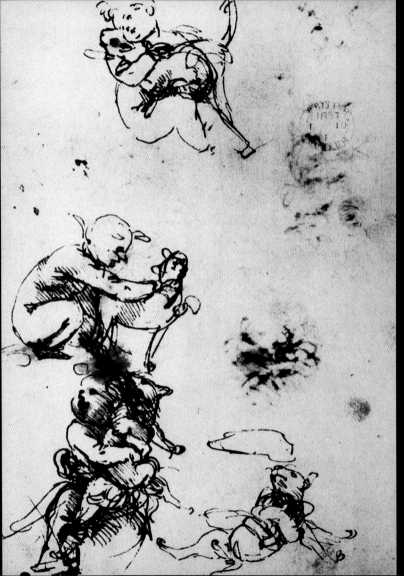

It must be universal for little kids to drag their cats around. Or in this case, because Leonardo did the drawings, bambini dragging gatti around. Capisce?

The smallest feline is a masterpiece.

–Leonardo Da Vinci, 1452–1519, Italian Renaissance inventor and artist

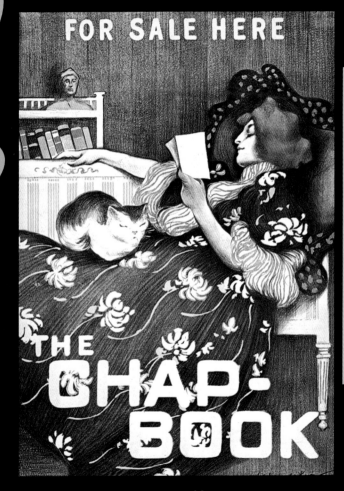

FOR SALE HERE

THE CHAP-BOOK

*L*eyendecker was one of America's most prominent artists. Smart guy, too. He did countless posters, mostly with cats. No wonder he was successful!

Cats curling up with ladies—a subject that transcends history, every socio-economic and ethnic group. The next best thing is being scratched in those little spots right behind the ear.

This 18th century print shows how the Japanese revered us. We were so spoiled in Japan, many of us changed job descriptions and forgot how to be good mousers. Some Japanese cats don't even grow tails anymore (bobtails)!

This one is obviously a good "window-watcher." *I* go out on the fire escape and watch all the ratty cats that go back and forth through my yard in Brooklyn. Sometimes they really howl at night, disturbing my sleep.

31

*N*ow this is a portrait of Peter the Great! People made fun of his European affectations (he wore a mustache and not the traditional Russian beard). That's why this 18th century Kazan cat has whiskers.
Get it?

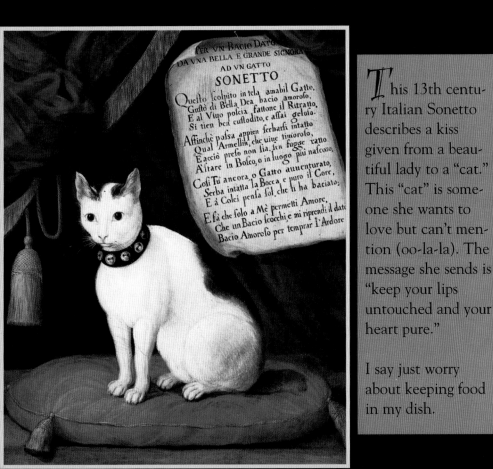

PER VN BACIO DATO
DA VNA BELLA E GRANDE SIGNORA
AD VN GATTO
SONETTO

Questo scolpito in tela amabil Gatto,
Gustò di Bella Dea bacio amoroso,
E al Viuo poscia fattone il Ritratto,
Si tien ben custodito, e assai geloso.

Affinchè possa appien serbarsi intatto
Qual Armellin, che viue timoroso,
E acciò preso non sia, sen fugge ratto
A star in Bosco, o in luogo più nascoso.

Così Tu ancora, o Gatto auuenturato,
Serba intatta la Bocca, e puro il Core,
E à Colei pensa sol, che ti ha baciato;

E fà che solo a Mè permetti Amore,
Che un Bacio scocchi e mi riprendi il dато
Bacio Amoroso per temprar l'Ardore

This 13th century Italian Sonetto describes a kiss given from a beautiful lady to a "cat." This "cat" is someone she wants to love but can't mention (oo-la-la). The message she sends is "keep your lips untouched and your heart pure."

I say just worry about keeping food in my dish.

There were once two cats of Kilkenny,
Each thought there was one cat too many.
So they fought and they fit,
And they scratched and they bit,
Till, excepting their nails
And the tips of their tails,
Instead of two cats, there weren't any.

–Anonymous

The Cooper-Hewitt Museum in New York City owns this delightful, "Catamaran" Lady and her family.

Here we go again with the kid and cat thing. Theophile-Alexandre Steinlen, more popular for his posters, painted this dubiously charming double portrait in 1889. There are hundreds of paintings of little girls and their cats. It was probably the only way to get both of them to stand still long enough. Never saw a happy looking cat in one of these paintings. Lily used to take me around the house like this;  she thought I would finally learn to walk upright. I didn't mind it too much; she always gave me extra treats.

35

Henri de Toulouse Lautrec, (1864–1901, French painter and litho-grapher) was normally in the dance halls with the prostitutes. With this kitty he became "unloose" Lautrec when doing this early painting.

Picasso's humanoid cat and bird was painted at the time of Franco taking over Spain. One could read the symbolic significance of power over the weak. Picasso said, "The subject just obsessed me, I don't know why."

I have never run after a bird, or anything else for that matter.

Cats are forbidden from chasing a duck down a city street.
–Law in Morrisburg, Louisana

$\mathcal{L}$ouis Wain, (1860–1939, British artist) is a casebook study of a person lapsing into schizophrenia. He started painting beautiful illustrations of cats, and they got pointier and more jagged as he got madder. This piece called "Feast in Fairyland" is a cat's tea party in a child's toy puzzle.

Bless their little pointed faces and their big, loyal, loving hearts. If a cat did not put a firm paw down now and then, how could his human remain possessed?

–Winifred Carriere, American writer

A law in Lemonine, Montana, states:

"Cats are required to wear three bells to warn birds of their approach."

I bet Tweety would have loved the Montana law. However, his repertoire of "I taut I taw a puddy-tat" would have to be revised. All I can say is, if they have time to make up laws like this in Lemonine...well...what can I *say*?

"But I don't want to go among mad people," Alice remarked.
"Oh, you can't help that," said the Cat. "We're all mad here. I'm mad, you're mad."
"How do you know I'm mad?" said Alice.
"You must be," said the Cat, "or you wouldn't have come here."

–Charles Lutwidge Dodgson (Lewis Carroll) 1832–98, English writer, mathematician, and lover of little girls (let's NOT go into this here!), sums up life.

*Cats talk with
their tails.*

–Cleveland Amory,
American writer

Cleveland Amory had three best-sellers based on his adventures with Polar Bear, a big white cat. This hero was found in an alley and adopted Cleveland, basically by refusing to move out. This wonderful portrait of the fabled cat is by the American illustrator, Lisa Adams.

I gave my cat a bath the other day...
he loves it. He sat there, he enjoyed it,
it was fun for me. The fur would stick
to my tongue, but other than that...

–Steve Martin (1945–), American comedian and actor

*Two things are aesthetically
perfect in the world—
the clock
and
the cat.*

–Emile-August Chartier, 1868–1951,
French author

A similar quote is: "In life there are two compensations—Prozac and cats." (Brian Walsh) Depending on your personality, choose your quote. It's the only interactive page in the book. This Kit-Cat® clock has been sold since the depression of the 1930s. There is a fan club with a creed!

Put a smile on everyone's face;
Love in everyone's heart;
Energy is everyone's body;
and Be a positive force in everyone's life!

If you want to join the fan club:
The California Clock Company
P.O. Box 9901
Fountain Valley, CA 92708

*M*aneki Neko, the Japanese symbol of good health and fortune, has a paw raised to greet customers to the store. Another legend says this is the replacement cat who scares away mice. Cat scarecrows work just as well, with less upkeep.

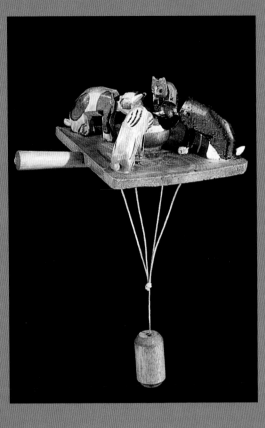

A dog will often steal a bone,
But conscience lets him not alone,
And by his tail his guilt is known.
But cats consider theft a game,
And, howsoever you may blame,
Refuse the slightest sign of shame.

–Anonymous

I never take anything, but my housemate Colette is a real klepto. She takes all the antimacassars off the bedroom chair. If she's already done that, and she still has urges, she takes Lily's underwear out of the drawer. She takes all the dinner napkins out of the closet unless Pearl puts a latch on it.

I don't know how they got these cats sharing one dish. I hate doing that with Colette. She takes all the juicy parts first.

46

Don't mess with your cat when you're stoned. He'll give you a look like, "Give it your best shot, man, I've been doing catnip since the day I was born!"

–Robin Williams (1952–), American comedian and actor

This cat, attributed to Salvatore Cernigliaro, looks as if he's been around the carousel one too many times.

" Felix the Cat, the wonderful, wonderful cat, whenever he gets in a fix, he reaches into his bag of tricks!"

What does this *mean*?

48

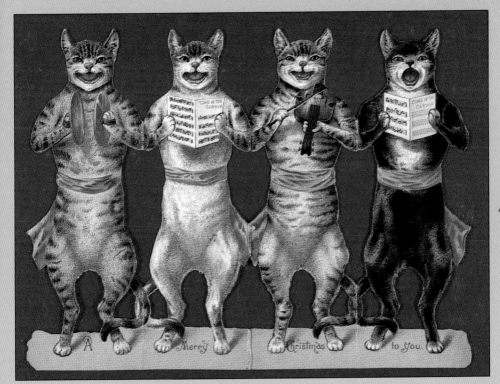

The more I see of people,
the more I love my cat.

–Bumper Sticker

Cross a cat with a man and you'll improve the man but deteriorate the cat.

Mark Twain

French novelist Colette (also the name of the haughty cat who lives with me) was famous for stories about cats. Here she is acting as one in "La Chatte Amoureuse" at the BA-TA-CLAN music hall, Paris, 1912. Some of her cats' names were Mini-mini, Kro, Kapok, Muscat, La Touteu, Petiteu, Pinchette, Minionne, Toune, La Chatte, One and Only, and appropriately, La Chatte Dernière.

He shut his eyes while Saha (The Cat) kept vigil, watching all the invisible signs that hover sleeping human beings when the light is put out.

–Colette, 1873–1954, French author

CAT PEOPLE

with
SIMONE SIMON
KENT SMITH
TOM CONWAY
JANE RANDOLPH
JACK HOLT

PRODUCED BY VAL LEWTON
DIRECTED BY JACQUES TOURNEUR
Written by DeWitt Bodeen

RKO RADIO

To be reminded that one is very much like other members of the animal kingdom is often funny . . . though I do not too much mind being somewhat like a cat.

–Joseph Wood Krutch, 1893-1970, American critic, essayist, and teacher

This 1942 version of Cat People, is the story of a young dress designer who is the victim of a curse that changes her into a deadly panther, who must kill to survive. A typical 7th avenue story. This movie promises "unrelenting horror" from beginning to end.

SCREAMING
TERROR!
...to
caress me
is
to tempt
DEATH!

The **CAT GIRL**

starring
BARBARA SHELLEY
ROBERT AYRES
KAY KALLARD

Produced by LOU RUSOFF and HERBERT SMITH
Directed by PETER HENNESSY
Screenplay by LOU RUSOFF

*I*n 1957 a young bride finds out on her *honeymoon* that she has inherited the family curse—a psychic link to a ferocious leopard—and numerous murders ensue. This beats "Honey, I have a headache" any day.

Cat Girl for the 50's...

54

Catwoman for the 90's!

Everything here is believable with the exception of the fur. This 1991 *Batman Returns* had the sexiest Catwoman. I want to point out one thing though: Cats groom themselves top to bottom by licking their fur. This maintains healthy skin and removes dead hair. Licking the fur and laying it flat makes it a better insulator. In warm weather, licking the fur cools the kitty. Cats also groom when distressed. So, enough said, where's the fur, Michelle?

No Catwoman ever had highheels like Paulette Goddard in the 1939, *The Cat and the Canary*.

Another famous cat lover was Madame Dupuis. In 1678, the celebrated French harpist left her fortune to her cats. Madame's sister and niece contested the will and won. There is no record of what happened to the kitties.

After Nastassia Kinski wore these contacts in the 1982 film, *The Cat People*, I'm surprised no one marketed them. In this movie, a beautiful young woman finds she has inherited a family trait; she turns into a vicious panther when sexually aroused. How's that for fantasy!

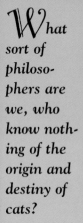

What sort of philosophers are we, who know nothing of the origin and destiny of cats?

–Henry David Thoreau, 1817-62, American naturalist and writer

I'd say the same sort of designers for these costumes. What's with the ruffle on Cecily?

In *Cat-Women of the Moon*, scientists land on the moon and encounter an Amazon-like force of female chauvinists (and this is 1953!). This movie is also available in its original 3-D format.

Cecily Tyson plays "Cat" in the 1976 *The Blue Bird*.

*N*a-Na-Na-Na-Na-Na-Na-Na-Na-Na-Na-Na-Na-Na-Na-CAT BABES! Now we're talkin'. We know "copycat" came from the Egyptians, which means babes have been wanting to be "catlike" for millennia. Here are two shining stars, Julie Newmar and Eartha Kitt. I think the latter actually is a cat, not a wannabe.

IF YOU WANT
TO BE A PSYCHOLOGICAL
NOVELIST AND WRITE
ABOUT HUMAN BEINGS,
THE BEST THING TO DO
IS TO KEEP
A PAIR OF CATS.

—*Aldous Huxley, 1894–1963,
British writer*

Cats as Muse

Bustopher
Jones:
The
Cat
About
Town

T.S. Eliot

Illustration by Edward Gorey

Bustopher Jones is *not* skin and bones—
In fact, he's remarkably fat.
He doesn't haunt pubs—he has eight or nine clubs,
For he's the St. James Street Cat!
He's the Cat we all greet as he walks down the street
In his coat of fastidious black:
No commonplace mousers have such well-cut trousers
Or such impeccable back.
In the whole of St. James's the smartest of names is
The name of this Brummel of Cats;
And we're all of us proud to be nodded or bowed to
By Bustopher Jones in white spats!

His visits are occasional to the *Senior Educational*
And it is against the rules
For any one Cat to belong both to that
And the *Joint Superior Schools.*
For a similar reason, when game is in season
He is found, not at *Fox's,* but *Blimp's;*
But he's frequently seen at the gay *Stage and Screen*
Which is famous for winkles and shrimps.
In the season of venison he gives his ben'son
To the *Pothunter's* succulent bones;
And just before noon's not a moment to soon
To drop in for a drink at the *Drone's.*

When he's seen in a hurry there's probably curry
At the *Siamese*—or at the *Glutton*;
If he looks full of gloom then he's lunched at the *Tomb*
On cabbage, rice pudding and mutton.

So, much in this way, passes Bustopher's day—
At one club or another he's found.
It can cause no surprise that under our eyes
He has grown unmistakably round.
He's a twenty-five pounder, or I am bounder,
And he's putting on weight every day:
But he's so well preserved because he's observed
All his life a routine, so he'll say.
And (to put it in rhyme) "I shall last out my time"
Is the word of this stoutest of cats.
It must and it shall be Spring in Pall Mall
While Bustopher Jones wears his spats!

Author's note: Bustopher is my third cousin twice removed on my mother's side. It's a family trait to know where good grub is.

*S*tretched pensively in noble attitudes,
Like sphinxes dreaming in their solitudes,
He seems to ponder in an endless trance;
With magic sparks his fecund loins are
filled, and, like fine sand, bright golden
atoms gild, with vague and starry rays
his mystic glance.

—Baudelaire, 1821–67,
French poet and essayist
from *Fleurs du Mal*

Balanchine *has trained his cat to perform brilliant jetés and tours en l'air; he says that at last he has a body worth choreographing for.*

–Bernard Taper, American author and biographer of Balanchine

Balanchine was the great Ballet Master of New York City Ballet after being ballet master for Diaghilev at the age of 21. He never did a ballet about cats though!

Stravinsky (1882–1971, American composer, born in Russia) and Balanchine had a great relationship for decades. They both loved cats! In a TV interview with Balanchine he turned and said, "Let's drink more Vodka and be drunk." Way to go Igor! By the way, they also collaborated on ballets such as *Agon*, first presented in 1957, *Apollo*, 1928, and *Violin Concerto*, 1972. With Valslav Nijinsky, the dancer and choreographer Igor wrote *Le Sacre du Printemps* first performed by Diaghilev's Ballet Russe at the Théatre des Champs-Élysées in Paris, 1913.

Hemingway and his cat chums. They stayed up all night keeping him company while he typed. He crossed imported Cuban cats with American cats and at one time had about 30 of them! He converted the ground floor of a tower into a sanctuary and allowed only his favorite cats to eat with him. Papa's cats were named after friends, authors, and fictional characters. Marilyn Monroe, Othello, Liz Taylor, and Zane Grey, to name a few. Still a popular haven for cats is his Key West house. You'll find there is a waiting list for one of Hemingway's cat descendants.

There are two means of refuge from the miseries of life; music and cats.

–Albert Schweitzer, 1875–1965, Alsatian philosopher and physician

Painting and writing, are solitary jobs, and it is understandable that these creative people keep the company of cats. Henry James wrote with his cat on his shoulder. I usually sit in a chair next to Pearl, but Colette always walks across the keyboard. In addition to Matisse here, drawing in bed while his cat stays warm between the feet, there are a few other famous types who lived with cats: Carl Sandburg, Victor Hugo, Lord Byron, Charles Dickens, the Brontë sisters, Edward Lear, Edgar Allan Poe, Dr. Samuel Johnson, Rudyard Kipling, William Wordsworth, Ford Madox Brown, William Carlos Williams, Richelieu, Christopher Smart, Beatrix Potter, and Shakespeare.

My cats died early on account of being so overweighted with their names, it was thought that SourMash, Appolinaris, Zoroaster, and Blatherskite...names given to them, not in an unfriendly spirit, but mainly to practice the children in large and difficult styles of pronunciation. It was a very happy idea—I mean for the children.

–Samuel Clemens (Mark Twain), 1835–1910, American author and humorist

Mama loves morals, but Papa loves cats.

–Susy Clemens, Samuel Clemens's daughter

The cat is above all things, a dramatist; its life is living in an endless romance.

–Margaret Benson, 1865–1916, British author

In 1937 all eyes were on *Stage Door*. Don't you just love the eyebrows on Eve Arden (she's holding the cat)? That's Lucille Ball with her hand on her hip. Newcomers Katherine Hepburn and Ginger Rogers made it big after this film. They're all actress wannabes living in the same boarding house. With a cat, *of course*.

I could name dozens of cats from outer space, but this one, Jake, actually played the role with Ken Berry and the perenially perky Sandy Duncan. Jake talked to Ken and Sandy through mental telepathy. Jake was also brilliant (of course) and flew a spaceship. In the end, *he* gets the girl.

What possessed Edgar Allen Poe (1809–1849) to write such a strange tale? While his wife lay dying of consumption, she clung to her cat to keep her warm. Poe was a great influence on Baudelaire, another ailurophile. During the Dark Ages, which must have been an appealing period of time for Poe, monks were great cat lovers. St. Patrick, the 5th century patron saint of Ireland reared cats. Pope Gregory the Great (540–604) had his only worldly possession with him in the monastary, his cat. Obviously, that's why he was called "the Great."

CARL LAEMMLE *presents*

KARLOFF *and*
BELA LUGOSI *in*
"The
EDGAR ALLAN POE'S
BLACK CAT

with
DAVID MANNERS · JACQUELINE WELLS ·
LUCILLE LUND · EGON BRECHER · HARRY CORDING
HENRY ARMETTA · ALBERT CONTI · LOUIS ALBERNI
SCREEN PLAY BY   DIRECTED BY   CARL LAEMMLE, JR.
PETER RURIC   EDGAR G. ULMER   PRODUCED BY
A UNIVERSAL PICTURE

*R*oddy McDowell loses his cool in the 1965 film, *That Darn Cat,* while cat is master of emotion. This Siamese helps FBI agent Jones thwart kidnappers. *They say* that cats don't mind being picked up like this. DON'T BELIEVE IT! It's humiliating to be treated like a baby.

*K*im Novak plays a witch in *Bell Book and Candle*, but in real-life 15th century Europe, Pope Innocent VIII (now there's a misnomer) condemned three hundred thousand to one million people to their deaths, because they were suspected of associating with the devil. These "witches" were usually outcasts, misfits with eccentric behavior who had as their only companion, a cat. It was thought that a witch could take the form of a cat.

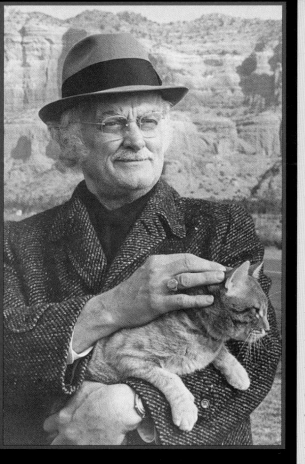

A cat on a leash, one of the most horrible concepts known. Tonto (the cat) had the dubious honor of leading Harry (Art Carney) cross-country after being evicted from their New York apartment. This 1974 film, *Harry and Tonto*, won Tonto a Patsy (Picture Animal Top Star Award). From the earliest times, cats were considered guardian spirits. The Egyptians felt that Bastet protected them from contagious diseases. They injected their children with drops of blood from a sacred cat. The cats probably helped keep disease away by killing the mice and the rats. Remember, it was after thousands of cats were killed in Europe that the Bubonic Plague came, carried by rats.

*T*his cool kitty was the star with his own trailer in the 1951 film, *Rhubarb*. He co-starred with Ray Milland, Jan Sterling, and Gene Lockhart. Ever notice how ginger cats make it big? NOT as big as black cats 'natch. Black cats have all the proverbs, too. If a black cat visits, good luck will follow. In England, a black cat in the house will save a sailor from danger at sea. In France, a black cat with a small white tuft is good luck.

82

$\mathcal{S}$assy the cat in *Homeward Bound* had the best line: **"Cats rule and Dogs drool."** My other favorite line is "Time to feed the cats."

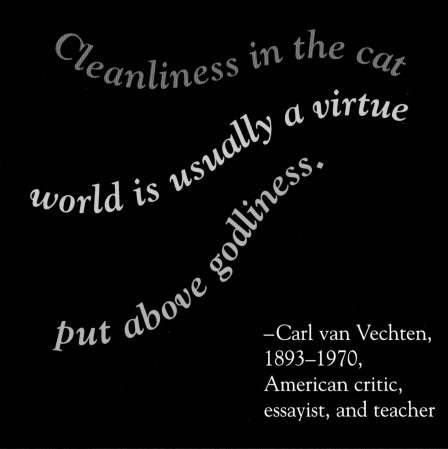

Cleanliness in the cat world is usually a virtue put above godliness.

–Carl van Vechten,
1893–1970,
American critic,
essayist, and teacher

Cats as
Myths

Villainy
Unmasked

....

A Fable from Aesop

A cat heard that there were some sick chickens on the farm. He disguised himself as a doctor and presented himself, complete with a doctor's bag of instruments. Outside the henhouse he called to the chickens to see how they were doing. "Just fine!" came the reply..."if you would go away!"

Aesop's moral of the story:
A villain, trying to act as an honest person, cannot fool a sensible person.

My moral of the story:
Order Chinese take-out.

European folklore has several tales of cats bringing good luck and fortune. In 1697, Charles Perrault published *Le Maitre Chat ou Le Chat Botte (The Teacher Cat or Puss in Boots)*. Everyone knows how Puss, who was supremely more clever than his master, outwitted the King into thinking that Puss' master owned all the land and the magnificent castle that really belonged to the evil giant, the Marquis of Carabas. In Brittany, this cat is referred to as the "Silver Cat." In France it's called "Matagot." This 17th century English chapbook engraving

is the English version of the "magician cat" also known as "Dick Wittington's cat." Dick's cat was used as collateral for a shipping expedition and scared or ate all the vermin in a potentate's castle. The potentate was so grateful he made Dick a rich man. These fables date back to Italian, Arabic, and Sanskrit tales.

I love cats because I enjoy my home; and little by little, they become its visible soul.

–Jean Cocteau, 1912–1970, French artist and filmmaker

Cocteau made this kinky kitty film after the Big War, in the mid-40s. I don't know if I'd want his visible soul hanging around the house.

Fritz the Cat grew out of the head of R. Crumb, the 60's counter-culture answer to Disney. Fritz became a movie star in 1972 in an X-rated, nonkid-oriented film.

Fritz was definitely the naughtiest of cartoon cats, including Ren and Stimpy, drawn by John Kricfalusi, and Tom and Jerry, Joe Hanna and William Barbera's first collaboration in the 1940s.

La Fontaine...

C'était un chat vivant comme un dévot ermite,
Un chat faisant la chattemite,
Un saint homme de chat, bien fourré, gros et gras,
  Arbitre expert sur tous les cas.
  Jean lapin pour juge l'agrée.

  Les voilà tous deux arrivés
  Devant Sa Majesté fourrée.
  Grippeminaud leur dit: "Mes enfants, approchez.
  Approchez; je suis sourd, les ans en sont la cause"
  L'un et l'autre approcha, ne craignant nulle chose.

Aussitôt qu'à portée il vit les contestants,
Grippeminaud le bon apôtre,
Jetant des deux côtés la griffe en méme temps,
Mit les plaideurs d'accord en croquant l'un et l'autre
Ceci ressemble fort aux débats qu'ont parfois
Les petits souverains se rapportant aux rois.

"There was a cat who lived like an over-pious hermit…"
Get a french dictionary to read the rest, this is a good story!

Global Proverbs

- Cat got your tongue?–*America*
- For a good rat, a good cat–*France*
- The cat is the lion to a mouse.–*Albania*
- Beware of people who dislike cats.–*Ireland*
- The dog for a man, the cat for a woman.–*England*
- The cat always leaves her mark upon her friends.–*Spain*
- If cats had wings, there would be no ducks in the lake.–*India*
- A cat has nine lives and a woman has nine cats' lives.–*England*
- If you want to know what a tiger is like, look at a cat.–*India*
- Handsome cats and fat dungheaps are the sign of a good farmer.–*France*
- Books and cats and little girls make the best furnishings for a room.–*France*
- A house without either a dog or a cat is the house of a scoundrel.–*Portugal*
- After a time, even a dog makes a compromise with a cat.–*Hungary*
- If a cat washes her face in front of several persons, the first person she looks at will be the first to get married.–*Early America*
- An overdressed woman is like a cat dressed in saffron.–*Egypt*
- The cat's a saint when there are no mice about.–*Japan*
- In a cat's eyes all things belong to cats.–*England*
- You will always be lucky if you know how to make friends with strange cats.
  – *Colonial America*

Cats in Many Tongues

ARABIC...BISS (MALE), BISSIE (FEMALE)
ARMENIAN...GATZ, GADOO
BASQUE...CATUS
CHINESE...MAO, MIO
DUTCH...KAT
EGYPTIAN (ANCIENT)..MAIT
ALSO, KUT, KUTTA
ENGLISH (OLD)...GATTUS
FRENCH...CHAT, CHATTE
GERMAN...KATZ
GREEK...CATTA
HEBREW (SEPHARDIC) CHATUL (ASHKENAZI) CHASUL
HINDU...MARGARAS
INDOCHINESE...PUSS
ITALIAN...GATTO
LATIN...CATTUS
NORWEGIAN...KAT
POLISH...KIT
PORTUGESE...GATTO
RUSSIAN...KOSHTS, KOT
SCOTCH...CATTI
SPANISH...GATO
SWEDISH...KATT
TURKISH...KEDI
WELSH & CORNISH...KATH

Cats as Vocabulary

Cat–Originally in the 1920s, Black musicians' jargon for a fellow musician, usually a man. The name was positive, like "cool cat." The phrase "hep-cat," was also used among the beatnik set. CAT Scan, stands for Computer Axial Tomography, not a cat standing over you with a magnifying glass. Cat and Mouse Act, passed in 1913, was to avoid the imprisoned suffragettes from achieving martyrdom by having hunger strikes. Cat-O'-nine-tails, is a civil punishment whip finally outlawed in 1948. Cat's eye– a reflector embedded in the road. Cat's whiskers– in the original crystal wire set, this was the very fine wire that made contact with the crystal. Cat's pajamas– a U.S. colloquialism used at the turn of the century, meaning something superlative. Is this how we have invaded the language? If you're really angry, are you in a "cat fight," having a "hissy fit?" A friend, David Frost, once handed over a memo saying "read this, but don't have kittens." If someone copies this book they are a "copycat," and when the deadline came up, we were all like a "cat in a room full of rocking chairs."

*T*hese fleecy buds grow to bunches of tiny flowers, thick at first and then coming to a point, and are so much like kittens' tails that they are called "Cat-Kins," which is the old word for little cats. You  can see by the picture how much the soft white buds are like Kitty's fur; and it is no wonder that the country folks should have named them cat-kins.

—about pussy willows, from
"The Book of Pussy Cats,"
19th century children's stories

> *Whenever the cat of the house is black, the lasses of lovers will have no lack.*
>
> – Old English Couplet